The Final Kiss

By:

Erika Latanya

Table of Contents

Synopsis

Prologue

Chapter 1

Chapter 2

Chapter 3

Chapter 4

Chapter 5

Chapter 6

Chapter 7

Chapter 8

Author Bio

Prologue

Let him kiss me with the kisses of his mouth; for your love is better than wine.

- Song Of Solomons 1:2 ESV

They say a kiss symbolizes the union of two bodies coming together in a harmonious relationship. It stands for desire, passion and most importantly... love. It's a token of taste and emotions.

The day that Ralph entered my life, Was new and refreshing. It was as If God himself hand delivered that man to me. I say this because Ralph was everything that I wanted.

He was everything that I needed.
He was everything that I craved.
He was everything that I prayed for.
He was everything that my heart desired.

So when God sent him to me, I knew that there was no way he could've been meant for someone else. We didn't meet one another in a traditional way and that's what made it all the better. He didn't have a cape dangling around his neck. He wasn't gift wrapped with a bow on top but I knew he was the one for me. My knight in shining armour until he came home. Smelling like… *her.*

Chapter 1

Wednesday

"So you're leaving me for her, Ralph?" I asked.

"Wednesday, stop tripping. I would never leave your sexy ass" Ralph scoffed.

"Then why have you been meeting up with her every night?" I whimpered.

"I've been meeting up with her because we work together. You know that" he smirked.

Ralph and I had been together for two years. Sounds like a long lasting relationship. Doesn't it? well guess what... it wasn't. The relationship was two years of BS. Ralph cheated on me several times with countless women.

"I don't know. How would I know anything? I just sit up in the house. Alone. At night. Waiting for you" between every pause and crack within my voice, I wanted to cry.

"Let's not go there with that tonight. She's just a coworker at the bank. Just like the others" he said.

As I stood against the wall, admiring Ralph's fancy denim jeans and fitting shirt, "That's what you always say. That's what you said about the last five women you cheated with."

"Wednesday, from the bottom of my heart, I'm sorry. I should've never cheated on you. It was a mistake. I was dumb."

He was and still is dumb as far as I was concerned. What man cheats on a woman who is good to him? I gave Ralph all of me. I cooked, cleaned and supported him. He worked at some mom and pops pizza joint when I met him. He didn't have a damn thing to his name.

"What's the point of apologizing when it's the same tired ass apology. Over and over again" I wasn't asking but more like making a statement.

"I don't know what else to say. How do I look?" he asked, ignoring my statement.

Lord, please help and save me from myself. I'm two seconds away from slapping the piss out of Ralph. This man practically disregarded everything I've been saying. I just can't take it anymore.

"How do you look? Why are you asking me? Go ask that little bitch!" I retorted.

Ralph looked good and he knew it. Why would I tell him how he looks? Just to go smile up in another woman's face? I think not.

"Aye!, she's just a friend from work. Don't go disrespecting her by calling her out of her name" he scoffed.

Did he really just defend this woman to me?

"Whatever" I rolled my eyes.

"How do I look? I wanted to wear my new Jordans but… I don't know. Rizz can't be out here looking like anything."

I hated when he spoke of himself in third person. *Rizz,* his name was in no way original. His mom named him after Ralph Tresvant. A member from the music group called New Edition. Yeah, he looked good. Boy, did he. His skin was clearly sun kissed and the smell of his cologne, smacked me like a hit of cocaine.

"You look casket sharp. You look good" I laughed.

"Thanks. I'm about to head out. She's waiting for me" he murmured.

Fuck her and fuck you Ralph.

"Okay. Have fun" I pretended to be happy.

"Are you sure that I look casket sharp?"

"Yes" I answered. *Yep! You're already dead to me mentally.*

"I'm about to leave but I promise I'll be right back. I won't be gone for too long" He mumbled.

"You shouldn't make promises that you can't keep. You wouldn't want to regret it" I shot Ralph a cold look.

"I'm serious. I love you Wednesday. Your hourglass shape, full lips, apple bottom, mid length wavy hair and brown sugar complexion is something I would never give away."

"If what you're saying is true then act like it! Show me some damn respect! Stop cheating on me!" I hollered.

"I'm not cheating on you."

"You may not be cheating on me now but you will. You're putting yourself in a position to cheat. This is how you ended up cheating with Michelle! Do you know how stupid this makes me look?!" I stormed off into the living room.

"Wednesday, calm down! I'm not going to cheat on you. Stop being so damn insecure!"

"Insecure! The reason I'm so damn insecure is because you made me this way! If you knew how to keep your pipe in your pants then we wouldn't be having this problem!" I shot back.

"Look, I'm giving you my word. I promise you have nothing to worry about. I'm a changed man. Give me a kiss before I leave" he demanded.

My silly ass kissed him.

"I love the taste of your lips. You always give me the best kisses. That's what captured my heart" he smiled.

And that's going to be your Final Kiss.

Out the door he went. While Ralph was heading

to go and do his dirt… so was I. I had a night planned of my own. *Let me call my little buddy.*

The phone rang…

"Hello" the person on the other end answered.

"Ralph just left" I spoke into the receiver.

"Wednesday, I thought you changed your mind?"

"Well, I changed it back. He's heading to meet another woman as we speak. I'm tired and I'm done with him" I spoke.

"Okay. How do you want it?"

"I don't care as long as she's dead. Tonight." I said.

Ralph

"Damn girl, you're looking good" I complimented Rebecca.

"You better stop flirting with me before I drag you into the back seat of my car and start straddling you" Rebecca responded.

"You mean like you did last night?" I questioned.

"Yes. We almost got caught by Wednesday. If it wasn't for my tinted windows then we would have" she giggled.

"You're right but it was soooo much fun. It gave me an adrenaline rush. I've never had sex with anyone near the presence of Wednesday. I usually wait until she's gone to work before I bring anyone to the house" I spoke too fast. I noticed Rebecca became silent.

"I know that you're in a relationship but it doesn't mean that I want to hear about it" Rebecca smarted off.

"But I wasn't talking about my relationship with Wednesday. I was talking about my past discretions" we were supposed to be heading inside the bar but argued instead.

"It's the same difference. I don't want to hear anything about any other woman. Especially while I'm pregnant with your child" Rebecca sneared.

"Do we have to talk about that right now?" hiding my feelings toward Rebecca was hard.

"Talk about what? Me being pregnant with your child? I assume you're still unhappy about having a baby with me."

"Rebecca, it's not like that. You and Wednesday grew up together. Once she find out that you and I have been messing around… all HELL is going to break loose" I was so pissed off about her being pregnant.

"Whether you like it or not… this baby is coming! So when and what are you going to tell Wednesday?!"

"I'll figure something out. Don't you worry bout a thing" I gestured.

"When are you going to figure something out? You have Wednesday thinking that you're hanging out with a coworker!" Rebecca rolled her pretty blue eyes at me.

I was mad at myself for knocking her up but I couldn't deny one thing. Rebecca was a beautiful blue eyed, blonde and petite devil. Literally. Rebecca was as cut throat as they came. She already had two kids by men she conned. She stole money and trapped both fathers of her children.

She trapped them by getting pregnant.

"I'm going to figure something out as soon as I get back home. Right now, we should be focused on us. We're standing out here in the middle of the park. Making a scene. People are beginning to stare at us" I pointed at the crowd of onlookers.

"Okay. Fine. Lets keep walking but I do have one question" she mentioned.

"What question might that be?" I asked, hoping it wasn't about anymore emotional BS.

"How do you honestly feel about me? How do you feel about this baby? Do you want to be with me? With us?" she questioned.

"I like you and I do care about you. I want children but not right now. I would never abandon my seed. I'm going to take care of the child. I want to be with you but not right now" I partially admitted.

Rebecca was not the woman for me. I didn't want to be with her. Ever.

"So what are you saying? What does that mean? Are you going to leave me? You're going to take care of of the baby and not me? You want to eventually be with me?" Rebecca rambled and rambled.

An older woman walked passed us. She reminded me of Harriet Winslow. I could tell she overheard everything the closer she got to us. She frowned up her face in disgust at me. She didn't hide her dislike of me, not wanting to be with Rebecca.

"Can we talk about this back at your place? People shouldn't be able to hear our conversation. You're starting to get quite loud and emotional" I whispered.

"Loud and emotional?! You damn right! I'm emotional because I'm pregnant with your baby! You got ME pregnant! You did this to me! I didn't lay down by myself. I didn't get myself pregnant."

"Yeah, okay. I hear you. I didn't knock you up on purpose. It was an accident. I thought you were still on birth control" my dumbass honestly thought she was. I couldn't help but wonder If she too.... was setting me up.

"I was on birth control. Everything isn't one hundred percent" she said.

"I know. But how often does that occur If taken properly?" I asked.

"Are you accusing me of trying to trap you? I didn't ask for this Ralph."

"I'm not accusing you but don't try and act like you're not happy. You couldn't wait to have my baby. You don't want me to tell Wednesday about it because you want to tell her. You want her to find out so bad... just so you can rub it in her face" I said, as a matter of factly.

"It's not like that and you know it" she lied.

Rebecca was always jealous of Wednesday. That's the story I was told and it showed over the years. I never knew why Wednesday allowed her to come around our home.

"If you say so" before either one of us could say another word... something in the atmosphere shifted.

My chest started tingling and my senses were picking up something.

"What's wrong? Why are you looking so paranoid?" she asked.

"He's got a gun!" I screamed.

Shots rang out at the park. Every bullet missed me. I laid to the ground until the coast was clear. I noticed Rebecca lying next to me.

Covered in blood.

Chapter 2

Wednesday

"Did you get it done?" I asked Roc.

"Wednesday, something happened" he replied.

"What do you mean something happened? Your job was to get her done. Your job was to kill that bitch!" I paid Roc to get rid of Ralph's coworker.

"Something happened and it threw me off."

"What the hell do you mean by something happened?!" If Roc only knew how mad I was. Too bad he couldn't see the imaginary steam blowing through my nostrils.

"I'm sorry" he apologized.

I leaped up from the chair I was sitting in, when I heard Ralph coming through the door. Something must've happened because Ralph was flustered. He paced past me into the kitchen.

"What's wrong with you Ralph?"

"I can't talk about it" Ralph responded.

Roc stated something happened. Ralph said he couldn't talk about what was on his mind. Either way, something happened within both parties and I was determined to find out. Somebody was going to give me answers.

"Yes you can! What happened Ralph?"

"She… he… someone…" he stuttered.

"Spit it out! Did you sleep with her?!" I needed to push his buttons. I needed his anger to release in order to get answers.

Picking up the glass of red wine that was on the table, I sipped.

"I can't talk about it but some shit went down tonight" he admitted.

"Shit. Went. Down. But yet you can't tell me what it is" I was getting ready to go in for the kill.

"You're not going to understand If I tell you. You're going to get upset and blow up" he claimed.

"I'm going to be even more upset If you don't tell

me!" I scoffed.

Ralph continued pacing around me. He denied to tell me anything. I opted to contact Roc once again. I texted him.

Me: Ralph is saying that something happened but won't reveal it. What the hell is going on? What did you do?

Roc: That's the thing...

Me: What's the thing? What happened? You better tell me something or else...

Roc: Or else what? Don't go threatening me!

Me: I'm not threatening you. I'm telling you. We had a deal! She was supposed to go away... If you know what I mean.

Roc: Somebody else did the job. Not me. I watched it play out.

Me: What! Who?! Why? And for what?

Roc: I don't know but it's done now. You said it yourself... that she's a con. I'm sure she had plenty of other enemies. Who knows who could've

done it.

Me: True. I just want her gone. I want Ralph to myself. He's mine. I'm not letting him go!

Roc: Look, I don't need to hear about your emotions. She's gone. I believe. Go live your life and be happily ever after. Lol

Me: Don't laugh. It's not funny. Is that whore DEAD or not?

Roc: I assume she's dead. Whoever did it left her drenched. In her own blood. I'm laughing for a reason.

Me: Don't assume. Is she dead or not?! Stop laughing!

Roc: I just told you. I'm laughing because I'm amazed at what you'll do for love.

Me: Don't judge me! You should be the last person to talk. You take lives for a living. You killed over a woman.

Roc: You're right. I killed because that woman was being physically abused. I didn't kill that man because I loved her. There's a difference. I'm not judging but I care about you. Ralph goes out into the streets and cheats. He does his dirt then comes home to kiss you. When are you going to finally say enough is enough? When are you going to finally say... "This is The Final Kiss?"

Me: I don't know but I have to go.

Roc: The woman I knew you to be... would never want to go this far and kill for a man. You're beautiful, smart and successful. That's why every woman is jealous of you.

Me: But I love him

Roc: Love isn't supposed to hurt.

Roc was right. Love wasn't supposed to hurt. I was at the end of my rope. I was tired.

Tired of Ralph and his BS.

Tired of his lies.

Tired of his games.

Tired of his emotional abuse.

Tired of him cheating on me.

And tired of him not wanting me.

Ralph said he loved me but that was a lie. How could he love me? How could he when he was making love to other women? And on top of it all...

I'm sure he wasn't using protection. I say this because I knew him. He didn't like to strap up. If he could do it bare with me then you know he was bare with others. Maybe I was emotional. Maybe I was overthinking.

But how can the reality of a man. Your man. Being intimate, feeling and tasting another woman not kill your own spirit.

I turned my focus back on Ralph, "What's going on?"

"Why do you need to know what's going on?" he smarted off.

"You left out of this house to go and see another woman! Unless you want to see your things packed and sitting outside… you better tell me what happened!" I was on a roll.

"She got into a fight at the bar. Some drunken woman approached her and hit her in the head. With a bottle" he lied.

Ralph's admittance rubbed me the wrong way. I felt he was lying. I hired Roc to kill that home wrecking whore. Not hit her in the head. His job was to leave her dead.

"I'm sorry to hear that. I apologize for seeming insecure. I'm scared of losing you again" I cried.

"It's fine. Trust me, you have nothing to worry about. I'm going to fix us some dinner. Let's eat and kick back. Maybe watch a movie or something" he smiled at me.

I decided to leave well enough alone. Something still bothered me. Something tugged at me in the back of my mind. I forgot to ask Roc about the one thing I had to know. I texted Roc again.

Me: I have a question. It's something I forgot to ask you. I've been meaning to but I was so focused on Ralph.

Roc: I'm listening. Are you sure you want to talk to me because it seems as If you're angered with me.

Me: Look, I'm not tripping about that. Just answer my question please.

Roc: I'll answer it when you ask me lol

Me: Omg stop playing.

Roc: I'm waiting

Me: Who was the woman with Ralph and what did she look like?

Ralph

Wednesday pissed me off to the max. Why couldn't she just let it go. Why did she need to know what happened. It was none of her business. Her only concern should've been about me and her. Who was I kidding. Wednesday had every right to question me. Facing my mistakes was hard to do.

How could I tell Wednesday what actually happened. How could I tell her that I had gotten another woman pregnant. I couldn't and I wouldn't.

"I wanted to make things right with us. That's all I wanted" I admitted.

"This fried chicken is good. What seasoning did you use?" Wednesday ignored my comment.

"I can't tell you my secret ingredients. Are you going to acknowledge what I said?" I asked.

"Why should I acknowledge it? I don't believe anything you're saying" she never looked up from her plate. Her behavior let me know she felt some kind of way toward me.

"I know. We can't work it out unless we both try" I reached for her hand as we sat across from each other, at the dining room table.

"Don't touch me! Keep your lying ass away from me!"

"Woah, Is that how you talk to the man you love?" I asked.

"I don't love you. Why would I love a man who cheated on me tonight?" she continued to eat.

"I promise I didn't cheat. You do love me. I know you still do."

"Maybe I do. If you want us to work out then you would tell me the truth. You wouldn't lie to me. You said I wouldn't understand. How can I understand If you don't tell me?" she asked.

"Fine. I'll tell you."

"I want the truth and I don't believe that half ass story about her getting into a fight" she said.

"We were at the bar. She had an old flame who showed up. He spotted she and I together. He walked over to us and started cursing at her. From the way it sound… she left him. He became angry and took it out on me. She came to my defense. We left the bar and he followed us out".

"Then what happened?" she looked at me with a side eye. Either she believed me or she could see I was lying.

"He shot her."

"What?! Really?" she questioned.

"Yes."

"Do you know how she's doing?" she questioned.

"No."

"You should go and find out. What If she made it ali…" Wednesday caught herself mid sentence. It's like she was about to say something regretful.

"I will. I'm about to go and find out. I feel like it's my fault. The guy thought she and I was dating but we weren't. We were just two friends hanging out."

Wednesday bursted into laughter, "It's not your fault. Things happen for reasons. Maybe she deserved it."

"What? Why would you say something like that?"

I asked.

"It's true. Maybe God is repaying her for something. You never know" she smirked.

For the first time in my life... Wednesday became a crazy woman in my eyes. Her statement was based on her feelings. She was so stuck on me cheating, that another human's life was irrelevant to her. Yes, I did cheat but we were talking about lives there.

"I don't know about all of that. I'm not a spiritual person. I don't believe in signs and wonders" I admitted.

"I do. I believe in them heavily. I also believe that people will reap what they shall sow" she stated.

"What are you saying? Are you trying to throw out hints?" she made me see her in a different way.

Her body language showed she didn't give a flying fluke. She was smiling and laughing. Still.

"I'm not trying to say anything Ralph. I don't have to try. You may not be spiritual but you know what I'm saying is true. What happens in the dark, will surely come to light. We've been together for some time. Don't you think I should be able to see through you by now?" she excused herself from the table.

"You can't just walk away. If I didn't know any better then I'd say you are happy about this. But why? What did she do to you?" my goal was to pick with Wednesday's mind.

"I'm not happy about anything. How dare you accuse me. Maybe I came off quite blunt but that's just me. You know that. It sounds to me like you're guilty. You want to turn this whole thing around on me. And to answer your little question... I'm not jealous of your friend. She hasn't done anything to me. Physically."

"Okay. I'm just checking. You're doing a lot of laughing and smiling" I said.

"Once again, it's who I am. Excuse me for not feeling something about it. I understand she meant something to you but I'm not sorry. I'll be sure to send flowers at her funeral" she said.

"Wednesday! We don't know If she died or not. Remember?"

"I'm sorry. I almost forgot about that part. I just have alot on my mind. I'm sorry If I offend you. I'm going to bed. Dinner was nice. I loved those sweet potatoes. No one could ever make them the way you do" she smiled.

"You're Welcome! I'll be glad when you make the baked mac and cheese. You know that's my favorite dish of yours" I winked.

"I know. I will one day this week" she smiled.

"One more thing, I love you. Things are going to be just fine between us" I stated.

"I know. I believe you. I have one more thing to say to you too" she said.

"What's that?"

"Be careful about the decisions you make. You wouldn't want to die regretting them" she stated.

Chapter 3

Wednesday

The next morning, I woke up to find Ralph gone. I assume he had gone to work. He had a corporate job with Turner Diagnostics. Happy, I was because he drove me crazy. I on the other hand worked for the Federal Government. Instead of working at a desk surrounded by nosey people… I worked from home at my own desk.

Roc never replied to my text from the previous night. I thought to myself *oh well. He'll get back to me soon.*

Instead of lounging around and waiting…

I opted to do some laundry. Not mine but Ralph's. That man stayed throwing clothes all over his man cave. I hated picking up after his sloppy behind. I was his woman so what did I do… I cleaned up after him. *Everyday he comes home and throws his clothes on the floor. How hard is it to place them in the hamper.*

I must've cursed him inside my head several times. The pair of jeans I picked up were heavy. I heard what sounded like change rattling. *At least clean the pockets out.* I pulled out pennies, nickels and dimes. I pulled out balled up paper.

I wonder what this is…

When I opened the balled up paper. It was hard to tell what I was looking at. It was dark. Black and white almost. It looked like a horrible science project gone wrong. That was until I realized I was looking at it upside down. *What the...*

A sonogram. Yep. You read that right. I was staring at a sonogram. It was a horrible copy but none of that mattered. Why did Ralph have a sonogram in his pants pockets? I don't know. One thing for sure is that it wasn't hard to figure out. When I read the mother's name of whom the child belonged to, my anger turned into rage.

Rebecca Arnold. That bitch!

I knew the baby belonged to Ralph. Rebecca was a whore. She was known for being a whore. *How could Ralph do this to me.* In the midst of my tears, Roc texted me.

Roc: Sorry for the late response. The woman was Caucasian with blonde hair. That's all I could see. I did some research. The woman's name is Rebecca Arnold.

Me: I know. I found out. The bastard has a copy of her sonogram in his pockets. I saw her name. I know who she is. Very well. So he was with her?

Roc: Yes. I'm sorry. I just wanna let you know... she's not dead. She's alive and well at George Washington Hospital. Do you want me to handle that, still?

Me: No. Let me handle it. I want this one.

Roc: Murder will change you. But you're not a killer.

Me: I am today.

Two people whom I thought cared about me, betrayed me. Everything was about to change and I was fine with that.

One hour later...
GW Hospital

"Hi, I'm here to visit Rebecca Arnold. I believe she's in the ER" I said to the receptionist at the front desk.

"Ms. Arnold has been moved to the second floor. Visiting hours just started. Head up to room 206 after you sign in" Gina, the receptionist directed.

"Thank You."

I headed up to room 206. Imagining myself doing the unthinkable was hard. Every time I pictured Rebecca with Ralph... the thought of killing her made me feel better.

"Good Morning sunshine" I greeted Rebecca.

"Hey, I'm glad to see you. None of my family has come to see me. I know I'm not liked but damn. They could've at least checked to see If I was still alive" she said.

"Well, that's why I'm here. The way I've always been for you. You and I both had a difficult life. Remember?"

"Yea, Wednesday. Your mother didn't turn her back on you like mine did. My mom chose a man who raped me, over me. Then called me a liar. I did later on steal from her but she deserved it. I was taking back what was due to me" she admitted.

"My mom died after my father left her. Left us. For another woman. You know how it feels to be left by someone you love, right?" I asked, getting to my next point.

"I do. I have more than one baby daddy. They all left me in a trailer park."

"Until I gave you the keys to the house I used to live in. You remember? The one I gave up to move in with Ralph?" I reminded her.

"I remember. You've always been there for me. You are my best friend and I love you for that" she cried, pretending.

"Then why are you carrying Ralph's child? My boyfriend's child?" Rebecca didn't say anything. "Answer me bitch! Huh?!"

"I'm sorry. I didn't know he told you" she said.

"He didn't. I found out on my own. He doesn't want the baby anyway. He's not happy" she stated.

"Are you happy? Do you want the baby?" I asked.

"I'm not happy. I do want the baby" she admitted.

"Well, that's just too damn bad. What made you think he would want the baby? Did you think he would leave me? You say I'm your friend and that you love me but you were ready to take my man" I said.

"It's not like that. Sit down so we can talk" she persuaded.

"No. I came here for one thing. And one thing only. They should've killed you last night. That was the plan" I stated.

"It was you?! You… You knew all along? You set me up!" she yelled.

"I had it out for whoever was sleeping with Ralph. I knew it was somebody but I didn't know it was you" I admitted.

"I can't believe you. Why didn't you kill me, yourself?"

"I was afraid. I didn't want to get my hands dirty but

I'll kill your dirty musty ass in a heartbeat. I trusted you!" I yelled.

"You can kill me but I wasn't the only one he fucked!"

I ignored Rebecca. I took the pillow from under her head. I placed it over her face and put pressure on it. I released my anger until I felt her lifeless body go limp.

Ralph

A few days went by since Rebecca was left for dead. I felt bad for leaving her out there. I also felt bad for not going to check on her. I heard through the grapevine that she died. She died. On top of that, Wednesday never breathed a word of it to me.

I wasn't going to breathe a word of it either. Moving on was the only thing that planked my mind.

"Happy Birthday Wednesday!" screamed the friends and family of Wednesday.

"Thanks, everyone! I'm so happy that you all could make it" she spoke out into the crowd.

Wednesday looked spectacular. The red dress she wore tugged at her hips. My mind was thinking of the many ways i'd have her bent over after the party.

"Happy Birthday, baby! I love you!" I shouted at her from the crowd. She was standing on stage. Being the center of attention. She loved every minute of it.

"Come down and open up your gifts, girl!" her cousin Ebony hollered.

Wednesday stepped down from the podium. Inching her way toward me, she whispered in my ear, "I can't wait to go home. I want you to rip this dress off me and bend me over."

"I was just thinking the same. We can either put everybody out or sneak into the back for a quickie" I suggested.

"We can't. That would be unlady like of me. But don't you worry, I'm about to wrap all of this up" she whispered.

I stood back behind Wednesday and watched her do her thing.

"This is nice. A Victoria's Secret perfume set. It says it's from Vanessa. Thanks Vanessa!" Wednesday acknowledged as she opened a few of her gifts.

Noticing everyone in the hall, I recognized someone. A man I never saw before. I thought maybe he was a relative of some sort. Since he continued being quiet over in the corner... I made a mental note to approach him later.

"Roses! Ralph, did you buy me these?" I choked. I didn't buy Wednesday any roses. The gift I bought for her was at home. Not the party.

"Actually, no. I didn't buy them. I have a special gift at home for you" I quoted.

"If you didn't buy these for me then who did?" she asked.

"I bought them!" a voice from the corner shouted. You

can just about guess who it was. The mysterious quiet man.

"Oh my, what are you doing here?" Wednesday asked him.

"What do you mean? It's your birthday. How could I miss your big day?" the guy responded.

"Aren't you going to introduce us to your friend?" I interrupted.

"I'm sorry. I'm a little startled. Ralph and everybody… this is my friend Rockford" Wednesday introduced.

"Everybody calls me Roc. You can all feel free to call me the same" Roc spoke of himself. He gazed into Wednesday's eyes heavy. He had a thing for her and I could tell.

How does he know Wednesday and who is he? She's never mentioned him to me before.

"So tell us, how do the two of you know each other?" I asked.

"They've been friends ever since childhood. Roc is Wednesday's best friend. She has him in her pocket" Ebony stated.

Ebony rolled her eyes at me. The rest of the party folks stared at me. Waiting for a reaction. What could I say after that.

"That's cool. It's nice to meet you" I reached out to shake Roc's hand. That's what a real man would do. I did notice how he acted as If I wasn't apart of the party. He was her best friend so he had to have known who I was.

"Well everyone, I'm going to go ahead and close out. I had a wonderful time. Thanks for coming" Wednesday addressed.

I on the other hand headed to the back. I needed to regroup. Alone.

"There's no need for you to hide out back here."

"Ebony, what do you want? Did you follow me to clown me?" I asked her.

"No. I came back here to tell you that you don't deserve Wednesday. She's too good for you. We all know about how you cheated on her. You're a dog and a coward" Ebony didn't disguise her dislike for me.

"First of all, you don't know what the hell you're talking about. Second, mind your damn business. Third, you're just jealous" I said. Ebony was bitter. Her baby daddy left her so she hated the world.

"I'm not jealous. There's something about you that's just not right. I can't put my finger on it but something isn't right. You're not right and I'm going to get to the bottom of it" she threatened.

"You're not going to get to the bottom of shit. You're going to stay out of our business or else…" I threatened.

"Is that a threat?"

"Ebony, take it how you want it. You're smart, you can figure it out. Just know that I'm warning you" I pointed my finger at her.

"You think you're all that. You think you got it going on but you don't" Ebony said.

"I know what your problem is", I hemmed Ebony up to the wall. "You want me. You're mad because you *want* me. You're mad that Wednesday has me and not you."

"Back up and get off of me!" she shouted.

"No, you like me being up against you. It feels good doesn't it. This is what it feels like to have a real man up on ya. Not that wack ass baby daddy of yours who never wanted you. He's never coming back Ebony" I laughed.

"Whatever. Either you're going to give it to me or I'm going to tell Wednesday" she threatened.

"You bumped into me and there's nothing to tell Wednesday. You know why? Because I'd never sleep with a skeezer like you. I knew you wanted it. It was all about catching me at the right time. You'll never get this D. She's your cousin for Christ's sake" I said.

I heard the door open.

"What the hell is going on back here?!"

Chapter 4

Wednesday

I walked in the backroom to find Ralph. Hugged up on Ebony.

"Wednesday, it's not what it looks like. He came on to me" Ebony tried to explain herself. I wasn't trying to hear any of it.

"Bitch! I don't believe a word you're saying. I know what I saw". I motioned down to my knees because I was in disbelief. I had to catch my breath.

"She's lying. Don't believe her Wednesday. She pulled me close to her. She tried to seduce me" Ralph tried explaining.

"The both of you are low down and dirty! I should knock both of you out but I'm not. I'm a better woman then that" I stated.

Naw, F that.

It took me all of five seconds to snatch that dusty, dirty and cheap ass wig off of Ebony.

"Get off of me!" Ebony screamed.

With every blow to her face, I unleashed a side of me. A side I never fully knew.

"Bitch, I'll kill you! You're my cousin! How could you betray me!" I screamed.

"Stop! Stop!" Ralph yelled, as he peeled me off of Ebony.

"I didn't do anything! It was Ralph! I told him to get off me!" Ebony cried. The weird thing about it is that I believed her.

Wholeheartedly, I didn't blame her. She could've pushed Ralph off. From what I saw, his body wasn't pressured against hers. He was more like...leaning. If I hadn't walked in, it's a possibility that Ebony would've given in.

"I believe you but only a little bit" I admitted.

"Why were you trying to sleep with my cousin Ralph?!" I asked.

"I wasn't. She was in here talking shit to me. She said I wasn't good enough for you. She called me a cheater and I called her jealous. I got up on her and I said she's jealous because you have me and she doesn't. I wanted to prove a point and I did" he admitted.

I believed Ralph but he was out of line. Way out of fucking line. If he could do that then what else would he do? How far would he have taken it? To prove a point? I knew what it was time for me to do in that moment.

"Ralph, at least you're honest about it". No longer did I want to be around those two. "The two of you can feel free to do as you please. Go ahead and live out your fantasies. It's over between Ralph and I."

I said what I said and I left it alone.

"Wednesday, please don't leave" Ralph begged.

"You should've thought about that before trying to bang my cousin. Today is my birthday. It's supposed to be special. It's supposed to be about me. And yet you're up in here showing how you really feel" I cried.

I walked back out into the dance hall. All the party folks were still there. They all stood and it was obvious they overheard the commotion.

"Ebony, you ain't shit! That's you're fucking cousin! You don't never let no man come between y'all!" Aunt Shuggy shouted toward the back room.

"Don't worry, I'll be fine Auntie. I'm not going to worry about it. They both gave me ridiculous stories. I believe they would've got it on If I hadn't walked in" I cried.

"She's just like her mother, May. May is my sister but that didn't mean a damn thing to her. May slept with five of my boyfriends over the years. That's why your mother and I were the closest until she passed. Stay away from Ebony" Aunt Shuggy didn't play no games.

Aunt Shuggy and I hugged. My keys and purse were already at hand. I said to hell with everything and I proceeded to leave.

"Wednesday, wait!" I knew that voice from anywhere. I forgot Roc was still at the party.

"Don't say it. Don't say you told me so" I cried.

"I would never do that. I knew one day you'd see it for yourself" Roc rubbed my back. I leaned into him and I hugged him. Sometimes in life a hug is all you need.

"I can't believe him. Why would he? And how could he? I know in my heart that he would've went further. I mean… was it already going on?" the tears wouldn't stop flowing.

"You can't worry about him. You can't worry about what's been going on. You're going to drive yourself crazy" Roc said.

I don't know what felt better. His voice or the way he made me feel safe in his arms.

"I feel so stupid. I missed all of the signs."

"Don't feel stupid because we've all been there" he stated.

"Sir, I think your services are done here. Wednesday will be leaving with me" I heard Ralph say.

"I'm not going anywhere with you. Fuck you! Fuck you, Ralph! I don't want shit else to do with you" I hollered.

"Just let me make it up to you" Ralph walked closer and closer.

Roc stepped in, "I believe she said that's all. She doesn't want anything to do with you, dude. Just leave it alone. Go away and leave her alone."

"Why don't you go away! Who the hell are you anyway? Wednesday, has never ever mentioned you. What's up with that? Y'all sleeping together?" Ralph questioned, becoming hostile.

"No, we're not. Don't worry about who I am. I'm the bogeyman" I almost laughed at Roc's response.

Ralph got out of dodge after Roc's remark.

Looking up at Roc, "I want Ebony dead".

Ralph

"I knew you'd come by to see me" I spoke.

She laid by the edge of the bed. Naked. Rubbing her pretty pink. Four rounds later and she still itched to ride me.

"She's my cousin but I've always had a thing for you" Ebony was beautiful. She was chocolate like a Hershey bar. Fluffy like a kitten.

Never had I been attracted to her. After she caused me to lose the love of my life… Wednesday. I didn't hesitate to go ahead and tap that. *Might as well since I was falsely accused.* My intentions weren't to sleep with her. I wasn't going to hurt Wednesday. Proving a point to Ebony was the key.

"Let's do it again" Ebony begged.

"I'm pretty tired right now. I have many things on my mind, Ebony."

"Is this about Wednesday? Why are you worried about her? She's probably sleeping with that Roc dude" Ebony said with sarcasm.

"Watch your fucking mouth! You don't know shit

47

about what Wednesday is doing!"

"How do you figure? I'm her cousin, remember?" she reminded.

Ebony had a point there. She was Wednesday's cousin. To me, in my mind, that gave me an advantage. Ebony was good for something after all. Information. I could say sex but that would be a lie. Ebony was horrible and basic in the sac. Wednesday on the other hand was a freak.

"What do you know? Tell me something?" I inquired.

"She's not what or who you think she is" she said.

"What do you mean, Ebony?"

"I don't know nor have the full story" she began to stall.

"Spit it out. Just tell me. Who have I been dealing with?" I asked.

Something told me that Ebony was out to stir up some mess. Trouble. I didn't mind as long as I got my answers. What she had to tell me didn't matter. Nothing could make me see Wednesday in a different light. If Ebony thought gossiping about her own cousin, would make me be with her... she was sadly mistaken.

My plans were to kick her nasty ass out. Right after she gave me the info I needed.

"She and Roc have been friends for some time. They're best friends, as you know. There's something strange about Roc. There's something strange about Wednesday. There's something strange about their friendship" she said.

"You can't tell me this information without elaborating. You have to give me some details. What you're saying right now, isn't telling me anything. I need more" I stated. I continued lying on the bed, watching Ebony.

"I'll tell you but I should probably start from the beginning. Hmm, let's see..."

Ebony played too many games for me. Either she knew the truth or she didn't. Nobody had time for her to look up to the ceiling as If she had to think long and hard.

"Just tell me" I demanded.

"Wednesday's mother died and her father left them" Ebony hadn't told me anything different. I already knew that.

"Yeah, I know. She told me" I acknowledged.

"I know but it's not true. She tells people that but I know what happened."

"Interesting. What happened and how do you know?" I questioned.

Ebony could be dramatic. What she said, was taken with a grain of salt.

"Her father didn't leave. Roc killed her father. You might as well say Wednesday did too. She ordered Roc to do so because her father had an affair. I know about it because one day I overheard them."

"Them who?" I asked, to be clear.

"I overheard Wednesday and Roc. I'm telling you this for a reason. You better watch yourself. They may or may not come after you" she warned.

"If they come after me then they'll come after you too. Right? Aren't you worried?"

"Ralph, I could care less. I'm on my way out of here. I'm moving to Philly in a couple of months. I'm going to be laying low."

"Ebony, what If I told you that Wednesday and I were just alike?"

"What do you mean by that?" she asked.

"Exactly what I said" I stated.

Ebony said nothing. "Come here and let me stroke you some more."

"Don't tease me Ralph."

Ebony was such a ditsy woman. I changed the subject so that I didn't have to elaborate. It's like she didn't notice.

"I'm not teasing. You came here to get what you want. Come here and sit on me" the rise of my manhood stood up.

Reaching for the condom on the nightstand, I put it on. The only woman I ever went bareback with was Wednesday.

"You don't need that with me Ralph. I'm clean. I

don't have anything."

"I don't care about any of that. There's more to worry about then just that. I don't want any children. Wednesday is the only one that received those benefits" I looked at her like she was crazy.

Ebony wasn't going to use me as a `get back´ to Wednesday.

"I'm ready. Move your hand. I can put it in myself" she straddled me. She tried to make me break but failed. I kept going and going. Like the energizer bunny.

I rolled her over on her back. "Do you remember what I asked you? About Wednesday and I being just alike?"

"Yes" she moaned.

"Do you know Rebecca?" I asked, in mid stroke.

"Yes. She and Wednesday were good friends. I heard she died."

"I cheated with Rebecca. Rebecca was carrying my baby. I set her up to get killed but failed" I admitted.

Ebony's eyes bulged out of her head. Terror filled her eyes.

"How did you fail If she died?"

"She didn't die right away, like I wanted" I laughed.

"Did Wednesday know?"

"No, She didn't but you do" I said.

"I don't know anything."

"You're right and guess what?" I looked into her eyes.

"What?"

"You won't be making it to Philly. The only place you'll be going to… Is the bottom of the river" I stated.

"Please, don't kill me" she pleaded.

"I won't If you promise not to snitch."

Chapter 5

Wednesday

"I want her dead, Roc."

"Wednesday, take your shoes off and relax. Ebony is not worth it" Roc reminded.

"I know but it's the point. She's always been jealous of me. She's always been envious. I don't know why" I said.

"People hate others because they're miserable. Her disrespect toward you has nothing to do with you. She hates herself" he said.

Roc caused me to want to look at myself in the mirror. *Do I hate myself? I murdered someone over Ralph.*

"I hate myself, Roc."

"Don't go there. Not tonight" he motioned his hand for me to stop.

"You're right. Ebony isn't worth it but I still hate myself" I placed the palms of my hands over my face.

"I murdered someone for love. For Ralph. Only to still not end up anywhere. Look at me" I stated.

"I am looking. You're beautiful, Wednesday."

"I did all of that… only for Ralph to still hurt me. To still cheat on me and with my cousin. What else is going to happen next?" so many thoughts ran through my mind.

"I think you need a hug. Ralph, is just a man. There are other fish in the sea. Don't feel bad for what we had to do to Rebecca" he said, holding me in his arms.

"We, I'm the one that killed her" I cried.

"We killed her together. I knew about it. Don't feel bad about it because she had it coming. She used people and she stole from them. You gave her everything. You took her in. You were kind to her. You were there for her when nobody else was. She made more than just a mistake. Men and women come and go but family is forever. She knew better."

"I'm a murderer and I'll never be able to live with that. How can I live with that?" I cried. The emotions within me tore me apart.

"I warned you. I told you. I knew it. I told you that murder would change you. I asked If you wanted me to do it" Roc brought back remembrance.

"I had to do it myself. It was personal for me. I wanted Rebecca to see her death coming. I wanted her to know it was me. That's why I suffocated her but I'm not a killer. I'm not proud of what I did. No human deserves to have their life taken" I admitted.

"I felt the same way you did the first time I killed. I didn't know what I was doing. I had no clue on how to cover up a murder. I learned from watching criminal shows. I took chances and made sure I wasn't seen. I didn't choose this life, this life chose me. I was afraid" he admitted.

"If you were afraid then why did you do it?" I asked, wiping the tears from my eyes.

"I did it because you needed me. You needed my protection."

"Huh? You're not saying what I think you're saying…" I hesitated.

"I'm saying exactly what you're thinking. Believe it because it's true" he said.

"You were like a pro. Every teen in the neighborhood was afraid of you. You hung around those gang bangers. There's no way... that my father was the first life you took" I stated.

Every time I spoke those words of my father... I felt horrible. When have you ever heard of a daughter wanting her father murdered? Never.

"He was and I regret it. I don't enjoy killing people. I never did and I never will. It was all for you and your protection" he said.

Roc and I both sat down on the edge of my bed. I leaned in on him to rest my head on his shoulder. The two of us sat still, looking out at nothing in particular. Roc placed my hand in the palm of his hand.

How could I have placed a hit out on my own father.

"Maybe I should've told my mother about my feelings. Maybe she would've understood" I hinted.

"Your mom was heartbroken. She might... MIGHT, would have blamed you for him leaving. She would've said it was all your fault. You and I both together, would be in jail" he answered.

"I mean… I don't know. I have no idea about what I'm saying" I admitted.

Why did my father leave my mother? Why couldn't he stay home and be a family? Most men cheat on their wives but they stay home. The smart ones don't leave their home for them home wreckers.

"Together, we both have to find a way to move past it. We can be better than the things we did. We give the people who hurt us, more power than they deserve" he preached.

"How do we move forward from here? It's hard because we are still being haunted. We killed those people."

"Look at me, don't cry. Everything is going to be alright. I promise" he said.

When I looked into Roc's eyes, I saw a different kind of man. A man I wanted to get acquainted with. On a deeper level.

"Roc, kiss me" I demanded.

Roc did as told. Fireworks let out inside my body. Never have I ever felt such sensation. He kissed. He licked and sopped up my lips. And my neck.

"I've been waiting a lifetime for you. To say those words" he whispered.

"You don't have to wait any longer. Take me" I said.

Ralph
Two weeks later…

Spending time with Ebony wasn't so bad. She was conniving and a nuisance sometimes. But I got to know her.

"What should I cook for dinner?" Ebony asked.

"You've been cooking something different every night" I laughed.

"I want to make sure you're satisfied" she smiled.

Ebony looked so darn good. The way she walked around the kitchen as she prepped, turned me on. A woman that cooked was always arousing. Wednesday cooked but her cooking was minimum.

Wednesday could fry chicken. That was fine but she barely switched it up. Spaghetti was the only other thing she cooked. I loved it all but I liked change. Whenever Wednesday didn't cook, I stepped in to cook.

But back to Ebony, she was a sight to see. She had on these leggings that tugged to her cheeks. Her cheeks were like two basketballs. Just bouncing up and down. She had a nice little slim waist with huge melons. Those melons were perky and sat up straight. Just staring at me.

I couldn't believe she went from being ugly to beautiful. I couldn't stand her. I disliked her but that may be due to Wednesday. Wednesday told me stories about Ebony. Stories about how She's no good. She used to tell me to stay away from Ebony.

I see why now.

Everything said about Ebony was true. Ebony may have been a screwed up individual but there was more to her. She had another personality that was different. I couldn't fault her for sleeping with me. I wanted it. I enjoyed it.

"I'm very much satisfied. Trust me. I'm satisfied" I winked.

"I'm going to make chicken alfredo. How would you like that?" she questioned, holding up a jar of alfredo sauce.

"That's fine with me. I haven't had that in God knows how long" I stated, never taking my eyes off her.

"Wednesday, don't cook for you?" she asked.

"I don't want to talk too much about it. She does cook for me. Sometimes but not much" I said.

Feeling like Ebony was going to become nosey... I changed the subject. Don't get me wrong, I liked kicking it with Ebony. But diminishing Wednesday wasn't in me and what Wednesday didn't do, wasn't any of Ebony's business.

"What does she cook for you? If you don't mind me asking."

"It's funny how you asked... knowing you shouldn't ask. You already know I mind. Why does it matter about what Wednesday cooks?" I inquired.

Noticing the frown on Ebony's face, I felt bad. My goal wasn't to hurt her feelings.

"Does she cook better than me, Ralph?"

"You shouldn't ask questions If you don't want the answer" I said.

Ebony stopped what she was doing. She shoved the sausage, pasta and sauce to the side of the counter.

"I want to know. Is she better than me? Does she cook better than me?"

I sensed Ebony was in some sort of secret competition. Who was I kidding... of course she was. She's been competing with Wednesday since forever.

"If you must know... I like your cooking much better. You have more skills. You enjoy cooking but Wednesday didn't" I admitted.

"Awww, do you mean it? You're not just pumping my head are you?" she asked, beginning to annoy me.

Women love fishing for compliments. Ebony knew I meant what I said. It's like she wanted to hear it again.

"Yes, I mean it. Don't go trying to make this a competition with Wednesday. This is not how any of this is going down. I like you. I like you alot. What you and I have is different from what I had with her" I looked to the television, in order to avoid eye contact.

Ebony started smiling harder than a jack o lantern. She was too eager.

"What we have? What are you saying? What is it that we have?" she asked.

"I told you that I like you. I do sense a connection between us. I feel like we have something" I said, while flipping channels.

"That makes me happy. But you know I'm still going to be leaving soon? Right?"

She asked me as If I gave a care. I liked her but I wasn't going to settle with her. Her leaving me soon didn't bother me. Reminding me that she was leaving wasn't necessary.

"I know. You should leave. It'll be good for you" I said.

"You're not going to miss me?" she asked.

"I'll think about you. Right now, your mind should be focused on new things. New experiences. There's nothing or no one here for you. Go on with your life and forget everything that's here" what I said was true. Apart of me dismissed her but it was spoken truth.

"You're right. I'm about to start boiling the water. I can't wait til it's done. I'm hungry" she laughed.

"Me too. What kind of sausage is that?" I pointed out.

"It's called Andouille. It's of the French culture. Originally. It's my favorite. Most people use smoked sausage but not I. You'll love it" she noted.

"I've never had it before. Since you like cooking so much... how about you go to school for cooking" I suggested.

"It's funny that you should say that. That's my plan. I want to move to Philly for that purpose. I got accepted into the Art Institute for Culinary Arts. I want to be a chef" she said.

"That's great! Why do you want to go out there for that? There's plenty of schools nearby" I inclined.

"I've been wanting to move away for some time now. Everyone speaks ill of me. I'm still young. I want to be successful. I want to prove myself and everyone wrong. I'm more than just a lay piece. I want to be somebody. Not just the girl who works at McDonald's".

I didn't know where Ebony worked until she said it. For two weeks, we never left my new apartment. Except to go get food and wine.

"I believe in you" I meant what I said. Wanting to

turn her life around, drew me in further.

Chapter 6

Roc

Still thinking about the sleepless nights with Wednesday, they were amazing. I've loved Wednesday ever since I've known her. The way she looked, the way she smelled and the way she wore her hair. I noticed every blemish and every change within her.

The night she asked me to take her... I couldn't resist. How can a man say no to her beautiful brown eyes. She batted those pretty lashes at me. Her eyes were so glossy that I could see a twinkle.

"I've really enjoyed this time with you. The most we've ever done was hang out. We've never kissed or remotely came to it" I admitted, while kissing Wednesday on her shoulder.

"I feel the same way. I don't know what happened. I was in the mood" she said.

Together we laid in her bed. Cuddled.

"Has it ever crossed your mind before?" I wondered If she had the same thoughts as I.

"Honestly, no. Ralph is the only man I ever saw that way. Looking at you in a different way would be cheating on him. I couldn't do that to Ralph."

It upset me that she would say that but I understood. Ralph was cheating and mistreating her. Who cares about If she was cheating on him or not.

"I guess" I sighed.

"I know what you're thinking. Although, Ralph cheated, I couldn't. Two wrongs don't make a right. I would not be laying in this bed next to you If he and I were still together" she stated.

"Just tell me one thing. Just answer this one question" I placed the palm of my hand on her thigh. Her skin was smooth like a baby's bottom.

"What might that be? I'm listening."

"Have you thought about it over these last two weeks? We've been spending much time together" I let my guard down.

"I did. Sometimes. Some days" she hesitated.

"I want to be with you, Wednesday. I want us to

be in a committed and serious relationship. I hope you feel the same way that I do."

"I'm about to get up and fix some breakfast" Wednesday removed herself from my embrace.

She rose out of bed, standing like a lost puppy.

"You don't have to be afraid. Wednesday, I'll never hurt you" I spoke from my heart.

"That's just it. That's it. You can't promise me something like that. I don't want to be hurt anymore. You can't promise me that you won't" she became teary eyed.

"But I won't. I'm saying something I mean. It's coming straight from the heart" I said, still lying in the bed.

Wednesday wore her emotions on her shoulders. She was sensitive and she hurt easy. Ralph was to blame for all of it.

"It's Ralph."

I shouldn't have been surprised at her response. She still dealt with the emotional break up. I knew she wouldn't get over him so soon. That's where I came in at. To take her mind off of him. Something I tried to do for the past two weeks.

"I know but he doesn't deserve you."

"Ralph said he'd never hurt me either. He too said he'll never cheat. Look at the things he's done" she cried.

"I'm not going to look at the things he's done. My focus is not on him. I don't care about what he did because I'm different. I'm not him. I'm better then him" I wasn't far from the truth.

"You can't say you won't hurt me. You may do it and not realize it. You may find yourself in a tempting situation" she continued to cry.

"I understand what you're saying but I'm a grown ass man. You're used to dealing with men that play dumb. Men that act like they don't see anything coming. I'm a murderer. I murdered people for good reason and I never got caught" I responded.

"Are you saying you'll never get caught cheating?" she asked.

"No. I'm saying that I've murdered people. That means no one can run game on me. No one can get to me or try to catch me slipping. I'm too smart for that. My intentions are not to break your heart. I sound cliche but please believe me. Just trust me" I pleaded.

"I don't know about this. Getting into a relationship could ruin our friendship. Don't you think?"

If it wasn't considered rude, I would've laughed in her face.

"Ruin our friendship? Are you serious? Being together won't be too much different from now. If it was going to be ruined then it would be by now. We're now having sexual relations. There's no turning back after that. We can only go forward" I said, feeling frustrated.

The only woman I've ever wanted, turned me down. In her own way.

"I like you. I like the time we spend together. You're a beast in bed. I don't mean to compare you but you're better. No one has ever pleased me the way you do" she said.

"I don't believe you. I've heard that so many times. You women always say that" I said.

"You have to believe me. Why would I lie? I'm not like other women. Trust me… you're the best" she said.

I laughed.

"Roc, why are you laughing?"

"You want me to believe you but you won't believe me. It's funny to me. That's all" I laughed.

"Hmph, I see you like to play jokes. Yea, you got me. I didn't see it coming. You are something else" she giggled.

"I had to give you a dose of your own medicine. So what do you say?" I asked.

"Ummm" she lingered, continuing to giggle.

"Will you be my girlfriend?" I asked, laughing.

"Yes, I'll be your girlfriend."

Ebony

"Noooooo, I want the purple one" I blurted.

"They're all stuffed animals. There aren't any differences between them" Ralph responded.

"There is a difference. They're different colors. I like this bear but it's yellow" I blurted.

Ralph came up with an idea for us to go to a county fair. It was about three counties away from where we lived. Queen Anne County, Maryland. The fair was a event I had little interest in but Ralph changed my outlook.

I never cared much about fairs. Often times, I associated it with little children and teens. The ferris wheel is slow. It only spins in one direction. There's no excitement to it. I like rides where I feel an attack coming on.

"You can have the purple one. You're probably going to bury it in a closet" Ralph laughed.

"It's going to be placed in the bed with us" I giggled.

The smile on Ralph's face was quickly removed.

He began looking at the people amongst us. As If he was searching for something.

"Are you hungry? I'm ready to go and eat" he said.

"Yes."

Together we began walking. We spotted several mini eateries. We spotted many stands full of quick bites. They all had something in common. Each line was long.

"It's jammed pack. Did everyone wake up with the same idea. Everybody and their mama is here at the fair" I blurted.

"I think today is the last day. The company is only here for a weekend. Those that didn't make it… are probably here" Ralph gave me a tiny bit of attitude.

"What's wrong with you? Why are you acting different?" I asked.

His mood changed after he gave me the stuffed animal.

"Nothing. I'm thinking about something" he said.

What was he thinking? What changed?

"Did I do something?" trying to get a good look at Ralph, I failed. He kept turning his head away.

I stopped in my tracks.

"Why are we stopping?" he asked, looking away.

"First of all, I'm hungry. We've walked passed about five eateries. Second of all, something changed. I know because I can sense it. Is it this fluffy fellow I have in my arm?" I threw the stuffed bear in his face.

He laughed and smiled again.

"Ebony, I don't usually do stuff like this" he admitted.

Ralph began rubbing over his head. Something was definitely bothering him. I assumed he was nervous, unsure or had a change of heart.

"Stuff like what? What's going on? Please tell me" I rubbed my hand down his shoulder.

"I don't take any woman out in public."

Here we go, I thought.

"I don't take any woman out unless it's Wednesday" he admitted.

"I understand but must we discuss her? Now?" irritated I was. He could never go a day without mentioning her. I know what you're thinking... how can I have a right to be upset? You're right. I don't have a right to be upset.

I was dumb to believe Ralph could get over her. I was dumb to believe I could slide in. As bad as the situation looks, I didn't intend for it. I did a lot of things in my past but I didn't plan to hurt Wednesday. Ralph was never on my radar. I didn't want him. I wasn't attracted to him. He was a murderer on top of it all.

I let my emotions get the best of me. Ralph caught me at a vulnerable time. When he stated I was jealous, I knew it was hearsay. Never have I been jealous of Wednesday. She was admiration to me. I wanted to be like her. She never seemed to battle with being insecure like I did.

Ralph pulled all of my cards. He brought out the witch in me but he also brought out the lonely girl. Believe it or not... My sex life was dry. When Ralph got up on me at the party, he touched something within. I wanted to discover how good he was in bed. See, it was just about intimacy for me.

Weeks later... there we were hanging out. In public. Being more then just intimate.

"I'm sorry If talking about her bothers you. She and I did break up recently. You were the cause of it. You have to accept the way I feel" He said.

"Excuse me! Don't go blaming your break up on me! I didn't touch you! I didn't go near you! You pushed yourself on me! Do you remember that?" I was mad enough to spit on Ralph.

"Yes, I do. I remember clearly. I remember you calling me. I remember you coming over to my house. I didn't force you. It wasn't the other way around. You had plenty of time to think it through" he said.

Apart of Ralph was correct.

"This is some foolishness. You wait until we come all the way out here..." I stopped talking to catch my breath. "You brought us out here just to start an argument. I could've stayed home. What's the point of being here?" I felt annoyed.

"Please don't pretend. We are not some happy couple. We are not a family. We are two people who betrayed someone. I told you about what I did" I sensed regret in his voice.

Ralph and I sat down at a nearby picnic table.

"What are you saying? You mentioned that you've never done this before. Outside of Wednesday. What is it that you want to do?" I asked.

"I like you but I don't want to be with you. I've done something I'm not proud of" he admitted.

"Rebecca had it coming. I know you don't want to be with me. I'm going off to school. You say all of this but I must mean something" apart of me was caught up in my feelings.

"Look, I'm just trying to get over Wednesday. I don't want to be cooped up in the house. You don't mean anything to me" he blurted.

"I must've meant something when you laid down and got me pregnant!"

Chapter 7

Wednesday

I never imagined being involved with Roc. How did this happen? How could this happen? Did I really love him or did I like him? What is love? Did he really love me?

Many thoughts plagued my mind. Roc said our friendship would never be the same again. He was right. Apart of me knew it too. After spending nights lying in his arms… I could never look at him the same. Especially because I'd be too eager to go for a ride. If you know what I mean.

Roc showed me a side I never experienced. He was a remarkable lover. The way he pinned me against the wall. I don't know If it was me or If the wall was too thin. Roc had everything within me and on that wall vibrating.

I liked Roc and I loved being around him. I wasn't in love with him. I second guessed myself on being in a relationship with him. I can't be with someone whom I didn't love. I mean… don't you usually love the person before claiming a title? I don't know. Those are the questions which ran through my mind.

Anywho, I picked myself up. It was time that I got used to my new life. It was time that I put myself together first. Forget about the old and in with the new. I said this because Ralph was my problem. I still dealt with the hurt he put me through. Getting over that kind of pain isn't easy. I tried and I forced myself to let go.

It wasn't going as planned. I only had two options..

A. Hold onto Ralph and miss my blessings or

B. Let go and be with the man who wanted all of me.

I opted to go with the flow. There was no need to rush nor overwhelm myself. I put on my big girl panties and out the door I went. Putting the key in the ignition of my Kia, I slipped on my shades. I turned the radio up and let my hair down.

I pulled out of the parking lot feeling like a new woman. Roc texted me while I headed to my aunt's house. She lived about fifteen minutes away.

Roc: Hey beautiful. I called you.

Me: Hey, I'm sorry I didn't answer. I was getting ready. I'm headed to Aunt Shuggy house.

I'm picking up a apple pie she made.

Roc: Yummy! That sounds delicious. Bring me some back. I'll see you later on tonight. Love you.

Me: Ok. I love you too.

I cared about Roc. I did love him. Platonically.

Once I pulled up into my aunt's driveway… I noticed something.

Ebony's run down Hyundai. *You've got to be kidding me. I'm not in the mood for this shit today.*

I had a feeling that I'd run into Ebony. Sooner or later. I kept my composure. I wasn't going to let no one run me away from my aunt's house. *Get what you came here for.*

"Hey, Wednesday!" Aunt Shuggy greeted.

"Hey, You should've given me a head's up" I winked. Aunt Shuggy knew what I meant.

"I didn't know she was going to be here. She just pulled up too. She's been here for five minutes. When I saw you pull up, something told me to come tell you."

"You didn't have to tell me. I can see that raggedy piece of sh…" I stopped myself in mid sentence. Ebony wasn't worth it. She wasn't worth my peace.

"I'm sorry honey. Just come inside and don't worry about her" Aunt Shuggy suggested.

I did as told. As soon as we walked in… there she was.

"Hi Wednesday" Ebony seemed cheerful.

"Don't speak to me! You know you and I aren't close! So don't act so damn eager to see me!" I yelled.

"Are you still tripping over Ralph?" Ebony had some nerve.

"Look! You two are not going to do this! Not in my house you're not! Y'all are going to sit here and eat this pie!" Aunt Shuggy demanded.

"I don't want to be here anymore" I stated.

"Wednesday, sit down. I think it's time that you two should talk" auntie stated.

"Is this why you called me over here? Is this a

setup?" Ebony asked.

"She called me over here too" I chimed in.

"The two of you have been at each other's throat for too long. No man is worth your relationship. Y'all are family. Blood is thicker than water" auntie stated.

"Ebony, you were wrong! Ralph was wrong too but we all know how you are! You sleep with married men!" I shouted.

"I know and I'm sorry. I've been celibate for some time. Nobody knows this but I'm moving to Philly soon. I'm going to school for culinary arts" Ebony stated.

Hearing Ebony trying to convince us she changed, was a joke. She's always switching career choices. She never finished anything. Her focus should've been on raising the child she abandoned. Her son lived with her baby daddy's mom. Pathetic. The baby daddy left her. I heard he comes around every now and then. Just to sleep with her.

"Congratulations but I don't care anymore. I've moved on" I said.

"Wednesday, moving on doesn't get rid of the

hurt. You have a right to feel the way you do. Just hear her out" auntie said.

"I didn't mean for anything to happen. I'm not attracted to Ralph. I wasn't after him" Ebony said, pretending to feel bad.

"Were you telling me the truth? That nothing happened between y'all?" I asked.

"I was telling the truth" she said.

"See. Nothing happened. Now, go ahead and hug it out" auntie said.

"Ummm, I'm not finished. At the time nothing happened" Ebony said.

I felt my blood pressure rise.

"What do you mean?" I asked.

"Ralph and I hooked up after your birthday party. We've been messing around ever since. I'm now pregnant with his baby" she said.

"You see that auntie! She's a fake and phony bitch! Look at her sitting over there smirking!" tears welled up in my eyes.

"I'm sorry about what I did. However, I'm not sorry about this baby" she said.

"Ebony, how low can you be?! You slept with her man and you didn't bother protecting yourself! Yeah, you're still a hoe! Get out!" Aunt Shuggy was ticked.

"Hey, Ebony! I know that baby doesn't belong to Ralph. Find another sucker" I said.

Ralph

"I asked myself what would I do? What would I do when I saw you again?" Wednesday snuck up on me.

"Hello, to you too? I forgot you still had a spare key. Since we're getting back together, you can keep it" I insisted.

"Stop dreaming! That will never EVER happen."

"So why did you come back?" I asked.

"You know exactly why I'm here. Don't play dumb. Did you really think I wouldn't find out? Did you think you could keep it from me?!" she yelled.

Standing still, with nothing to say, "I don't know what you're talking about, Wednesday."

I lied. Ebony is the only thing she could've been talking about.

"Go ahead! Keep lying! Where is she?! Tell her to come out!" Wednesday lashed out.

"Stop looking through my house! If you're not here for ME, then leave. Go back home to your little boyfriend. The man you've been cheating on me with" I inclined.

"Don't you dare go there! Roc has nothing to do with this! I have never ever cheated on you! You're so full of shi… Where is she?!" she continued.

"I don't know who or what you're talking about. If you don't want to be with me then leave. I will not stand here and allow you to accuse me, Wednesday."

"You're such an actor. Accuse you? You've been lying and cheating on me. I can't accuse you of something that's not true. How long" she asked.

I should've known things would spiral out of control. I lied with all my might but Wednesday knew. Lying to the woman you love, leaves you feeling awful. Wednesday was devastated. She whimpered and placed the palms of her hands over her face. I felt bad. I felt like an asshole. Wednesday was too good for me.

I didn't deserve her.

"I'm sorry Wednesday. I really truly am. None of this was meant to happen. It's not what you think" I walked closer to her.

"Don't come near me! Tell me what I'm thinking! Don't play me! Don't make me out to be crazy. Tell me the truth. I want the beginning and the end!"

"I didn't begin sleeping with Ebony until after the party. Never have I ever touched her since you and I were together" I admitted.

"Damn all of that Ralph! None of that matters!" Wednesday paced my living room floor.

Watching snot run down her nose saddened me. She was hurt but also cute. I've never seen a woman look beautiful even while she was hurt. That's another reason I loved her. Wednesday was a natural beauty. Inside and out. At every stage of her emotion. Apart of me wanted to tick her off just so I could see a beautiful tear.

I may sound crazy but you'd have to see her in order to understand.

"I'm sorry" I didn't know what else to say. I messed up.

"Sorry won't change anything. Sorry won't undo the pain. The pain you caused. You can look at me any kind of way you want. I know I'm fussing at you and I'm going to keep on doing it. You're going to listen to what I have to say!"

I'm sorry that I angered her. I'm sorry that I rolled my eyes at her. I can't deal with people putting me in my place. I can't deal with people telling me I did wrong. I knew that I messed up but the reminder didn't help me. If things had been my way then I would've apologized and Wednesday and I would've moved on happily.

"I didn't intend for Ebony to get pregnant."

"Well, it's just a little too late for that now. You made the choice to be a father when you laid down with her. I don't want to talk about this anymore. I'm done with this and you. I have to go."

Wednesday brushed past me. "Wait. Please don't go. Wednesday, just hear me out. I'm still..."

"No! There's nothing left to say! I did everything for you! I cooked, cleaned, and I loved you! Then Rebecca" she cried.

The situation turned sour by the moment. I didn't miss the mentioning of Rebecca's name.

"I still love you. What about Rebecca? What are you saying? What did you do?" I asked.

"I did it" she began to speak.

"You did what?" I asked.

"She wasn't completely dead. I finished her off in the hospital" she cried.

"How did you kill her, when I did?" I asked.

"What? Stop lying. How did you kill her?" she asked me.

"I had it all set up. I wasn't about to let Rebecca ruin you and I. I wasn't going to raise that bastard baby of hers" I laughed.

"Getting Ebony pregnant didn't make things better. Rebecca wasn't dead. I smothered her. I too, wasn't going to let her have that baby" she cried.

"There's no sense in talking about that. You and I can fix this together. We can get rid of Ebony and be together. Nothing can keep us apart now. We have another chance" I said.

"Man bye! I will never again in life be with you! I almost ruined my entire life for you! I didn't kill Rebecca for you! Or to keep you! I killed her because

I was angry! I wanted her gone. But um… I never knew you were a killer. I'm done. Move out of my way."

"Wednesday! Don't leave. I'm not a real killer. I did it for us" I pleaded.

"Ralph, look at yourself. I'm never coming back. I didn't feel good about what I did. I did all of that and it backfired on me. Killing Rebecca didn't get rid of our problems. I killed one baby and you created another. I lost myself over you. I'll never do that again. Y'all weren't worth the stress. Of all women, you got my cousin pregnant. You're the center of it all. Rest in hell!"

"The baby isn't mine. I got snipped right after Rebecca died. Ebony better track down her raggedy ass baby daddy. If it makes you feel any better… I'm going to kill her" I said.

"I don't care. I'm moving on with my life. Being snipped is not one hundred percent. Raise your child and be happy. Killing them won't bring me back. Goodbye Ralph."

Chapter 8

Wednesday

Police in Prince George's County say a man killed his girlfriend before killing himself at their Prince George's County home in an apparent murder-suicide last night.

Officers say they responded to a town home on the 7800 block of Pinewood Court in the Clinton area around 11:48 p.m.Tuesday. They say a neighbor discovered the bodies of pregnant 29-year-old Ebony Green, and her boyfriend, 29-year-old Ralph Scott dead inside. The front door was left unlocked.

Police believe Ralph Scott attacked his girlfriend, causing trauma to her upper body, then shot her before shooting himself.

Officers did not find any signs of forced entry and say there does not seem to be any threat to the public at this time. However, the child Ebony Scott was carrying, did not survive. The investigation is continuing.

"Dang! He finally went crazy, huh?" Roc's loud mouth startled me.

"Don't sneak up on me like that. I'm not surprised. He hinted around that he would do something. I wasn't expecting suicide. I don't know how I feel about it. I'm numb to the entire situation. I want to move on away from it" I exhaled.

"I understand. Right now you're venting. What do you mean by... he hinted around? Did you go and see him?" I knew Roc would ask me that.

"Yes, I did. I went to confront him about Ebony. I wanted to know If it was true. The whole baby thing. His nasty ass had the nerve, to beg me to stay. I told him it was over. You'll never guess what else?" I glared at Roc.

"What else? Tell me" he stood against the kitchen island.

"The reason why our attempt to kill Rebecca failed... was because of him. Ralph put out a hit on her too. The same night" I shook my head in disbelief.

"Wow! Nobody liked Rebecca. She ruined lives" Roc laughed.

"He said that he did it for me. He didn't want the

baby she was carrying. What the heck was he thinking? He slept with my cousin. A family member. Someone who I've never seen eye to eye with. He can't say it was a mistake. He willingly got involved after the party. Not just any party but my birthday party. He can go to hell" I exhaled.

"Trust me, he's already there. He's out of your life forever now. All he did was mistreat you. He cheated on you with several women" Roc reminded me.

"Don't remind me. I lived with that everyday. I stayed with him because he was there. He was my boyfriend. Speaking of boyfriend... they called Ebony is girlfriend on the news. How pathetic and hilarious is that" I exhaled.

"Fox 5 has always been known for reporting false news. They don't check factual information first" together we laughed at Roc's comment.

"True. I stayed because I had a title. Finally, I wasn't single anymore" I exhaled.

"Just because he was your man, didn't mean you weren't single. He was there physically. He wasn't there mentally and emotionally. You didn't want to be lonely but you were. Many nights you called me crying. He didn't always come home. He made two babies on you. He wasn't the man for you" he said.

"I just want to move on. He claimed the baby wasn't his. He claimed to be snipped. I don't believe that. I want a new life. As much as I despise him... I'm sad that he died" I whimpered.

"It's normal to feel something for his death. Remember, he chose to die. He made mistakes he couldn't handle. He did what he wanted without thinking about the consequences. It's time for you to live your life now" he stated.

"Trust me I am" I replied, stretching out on the living room couch.

"I'm glad you said that. I want to be apart of your moving on. I still want to be with you" Roc sat in front of me on the couch. Interrupting my space.

"We talked about this already" I said.

"Wednesday, will you marry me?" I rose from the couch, pacing the floor.

"No. I can't do that. I'm leaving you behind too. I don't want any memory of you or this place. When I say you... I mean the murders. I can't anymore. I want a new life" I exhaled.

"I can't let you do that. I can't let you walk out of that door. If I do then it means I have to kill you" he said.

"What?" I asked out of confusion.

"You have information on me. How do I know you won't turn me in? You could pin everything on me" he said.

"Roc, how could you? Why would you kill me? We've been friends for years. I would never turn you in. You know what, I'm done. You're going to let me walk out of this door. You're not going to chase me or harm me. You're going to let me and the thought of us being together...go. Understood?" I demanded my freedom.

"Understood" he agreed.

"Goodbye Roc" I left and I never looked back.

As I sat in my car, I felt like a new individual. I felt free. I turned my life upside down over a man. A man who didn't love me. All of that was about to change. I took my life back. As far as Roc goes, I wasn't going to turn him in. I had another plan for him.

I dialed a familiar number.

"Hello" I answered.

"How do you feel?"

"I feel good. It's all over now" I spoke into the receiver.

"Good. Girl, you almost killed me."

"Rebecca, I had to play it out. Thanks for being there for me" I said.

"Pretending to be pregnant and dead was hard" Rebecca said.

"I know. I knew he'd fall for it. It was stupid of me to do this. Ralph wasn't worth it. No man is worth it. I may be moving on but I'll still have the thoughts. Our plan almost backfired until Ebony. I knew she'd say something to him. Come on to him. That's how she was. She sealed the deal by being herself. A hoe. I love when trash take itself out. I knew he'd kill her. Ralph couldn't live with what he had done to me. He was weak" I said.

"He loved you and his fun too. What an ass" she

said.

"Not anymore. This is what happens when you keep cheating. He cheated then came home to kiss me. That was his Final Kiss" I spoke.

"Right. What do we do now?" she asked.

"I don't know but I need you to handle Roc. He threatened to kill me. I turned down his marriage proposal. He thinks I'll turn him in but he might try and turn me in" I said.

"Don't worry. I'll handle him with a lighter and a match. He and that house is going to burn to a crisp" she said.

"That's what friends are for" I said.

The End...

Author Bio

Erika Latanya is a serial storyteller who hails from the Washington, D.C. metro area. Her love for writing started at the early age of 8yrs old when she received her very first diary. From then on, she penned short stories and poetry. Erika expresses that writing is a form of therapy. It gives her the opportunity to express and share her imagination with the world.

Keep in touch

www.twitter.com/erikalatanya

www.instagram.com/erikalatanya

www.facebook.com/erikalatanyabooks

www.erikalatanya.com